IMAGES OF WAR
NORMANDY 1944
THE BATTLE OF THE HEDGEROWS

The *bocage*—the Americans called it the 'hedgerows'—allowed German defenders to frustrate First Army's attacks for nearly two months. Bradley called it 'a line of defense more formidable than any even Rommel could have contrived.'

IMAGES OF WAR

NORMANDY 1944
THE BATTLE OF THE HEDGEROWS

SIMON FORTY

Pen & Sword
MILITARY

First published in Great Britain in 2018 by
PEN & SWORD MILITARY
an imprint of
Pen & Sword Books Ltd,
47 Church Street,
Barnsley,
South Yorkshire.
S70 2AS

A CIP record for this book is available from the
British Library.

ISBN 978 1 52672 371 0

Printed and bound by CPI UK

Pen & Sword Books Ltd incorporates the
Imprints of Pen & Sword Aviation, Pen & Sword
Maritime,
Pen & Sword Military, Wharncliffe Local History,
Pen & Sword Select, Pen & Sword Military
Classics and Leo Cooper.

For a complete list of Pen & Sword titles please
contact
Pen & Sword Books Limited
47 Church Street, Barnsley, South Yorkshire, S70
2AS, England
E-mail: enquiries@pen-and-sword.co.uk
Website: www.pen-and-sword.co.uk

Abbreviations

CCA/B/R Combat Command A/B/R
CG commanding general
CLY County of London Yeomanry
CP command post
ECB Engineer Combat Battalion
FA field artillery
FJR *Fallschirmjäger* = German paratrooper
GR *Grenadier Regiment* (German infantry)
KG *Kampfgruppe* = battle group, ersatz
combinations of troops that happened to be
available at a given time. Usually named for their
commander
OB West *Oberbefehlshaber West* = C-in-C
West
OKH *Oberkommando des Heeres* = Army High
Command
OT Organisation Todt
PIR parachute infantry regiment
PzGr *Panzergrenadier* = armoured infantry
RCT regimental combat team
RHA Royal Horse Artillery
(SS-) sPzAbt (SS-) *schwere Panzer-Abteilung* =
heavy tank battalion (Tiger Is or IIs)
SdKfz *Sonderkraftfahrzeug* = special purpose
vehicle
TD tank destroyer—could mean towed antitank
guns or tracked (M10, M18 or M36)

Note

Dates are 1944 unless specified otherwise.

Photographic Sources

The photographs in this book are predominantly
from US National Archives. They have been
sourced via Battlefield Historian, without whom
this book could not have been undertaken or
direct from National Archives, College Park,
Maryland. Captioning is always made easier with
reference to Photosnormandie's excellent Flickr
photostream. The US official maps are from the
various 'Green Books' which can be found online
at the US Army Center of Military History.

Contents

The countryside of southern England, particularly Dorset, Devon and Cornwall, is very similar to that of Normandy, as is the climate. **Above**, an incident at Kingsbridge; **Below**, training at Torcross, both locations in Devon. Note the hedgerows, and the sunken lane.

Introduction

Did the Allied planners spend too much time worrying about the beachheads and too little thinking about how they were going to fight inland through the bocage? It's a good question and one that's difficult to answer. Training in the fields of Great Britain, with its own version of the hedgerows, was certainly as close to the real thing as one could get outside France. Perhaps a better question is whether the Allies' operational and tactical doctrine was deficient. It is often suggested that German tactics and NCO-level leadership were better than those of the Allies. Unsurprisingly, this might well have been true when green Allied units were blooded for the first time—such as the 90th Infantry Division, who started badly but would go on to live up to their 'Tough 'Ombres' nickname. Attrition, however, was a great leveller, and the Germans were losing as many or more men than the Americans. It's also difficult to compare like for like when one side executed one soldier for desertion while the other despatched anywhere from 15,000 to 50,000 depending on whose figures you believe. And while the Germans tactics may have been good, their strategic decision-making, particularly with Hitler at the helm, was no match for the Allies.

Was the German equipment better than the Allies? For many years opinion on this has ranged decidedly in the favour of the Germans. At the time questions were asked in the House of Commons by MP Major Richard Stokes about what were seen as substandard British tanks. (One waggish MP queried: 'Will the Prime Minister be prepared to take charge of a Churchill tank and allow the Hon. Member for Ipswich [Stokes] to take charge of a Tiger tank?') In *A Soldier's Story*, Bradley emphasises the disparity: 'the Tiger could both outgun and outduel any Allied tank in the field.' But the thing was that there weren't many Tigers, and those that were in Normandy were ranged against the British and Commonwealth troops who had the Sherman Firefly and were developing better antitank ammunition. The most numerous German AFVs were the PzKpfw IV and StuG III, both of which were no better than the Allied Shermans, although the Panther was. But tanks are only as good as their crews—as von Manteuffel's inexperienced Panther crews discovered at Arracourt—and an awful lot of the veteran German crews were dying. On the other hand, Allied artillery, much more significant than armour in the hedgerow battles, was certainly better, more numerous, more accurate and, crucially, very effective. So too was Allied transport: as opposed to much of the German Army in 1944 which still used horses.

The battle of Normandy, pored over for 75 years, still prompts many questions. In the end, however, the qualitative differences between the equipment and the men is irrelevant. The Battle of the Hedgerows posed significant problems for the US Army, questions they answered. They won. Emphatically. They gained the initiative and held it. From the morning of 6 June when Allied paratroopers landed, the Germans were reactive, unable to take the initiative. First the cutting of the Cotentin, then the attack on Cherbourg, then the July offensive towards Saint-Lô: the Germans' only attempt to gain the initiative was when Panzer Lehr and 2nd SS-Panzer Division—neither at full strength—attacked the St-Fromond bridgehead. The attack was shrugged off, those Panzers that weren't destroyed by ground or air forces retreated to be decimated a few days later in the bombing that started Operation Cobra. Holding the initiative may not win you the war, but it gives you the chance to do so. Bradley seized the opportunity, and the result was a victory that broke the German hold on France.

Below: Held up in the bocage and around Caen with force levels at stalemate, the Allies needed to expand their foothold in France and bring their mobile forces into play.

Right: Perfect ambush country, the bocage allowed the German defenders to hold off the better-armed, more numerous Allied forces.

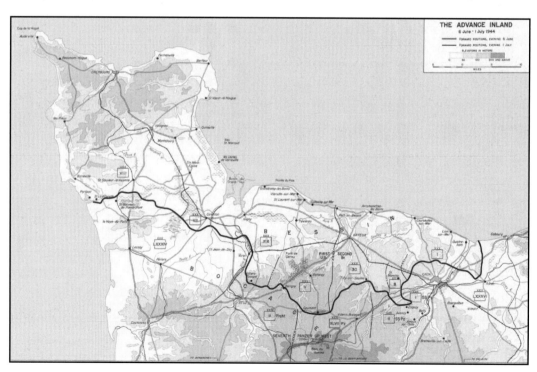

8

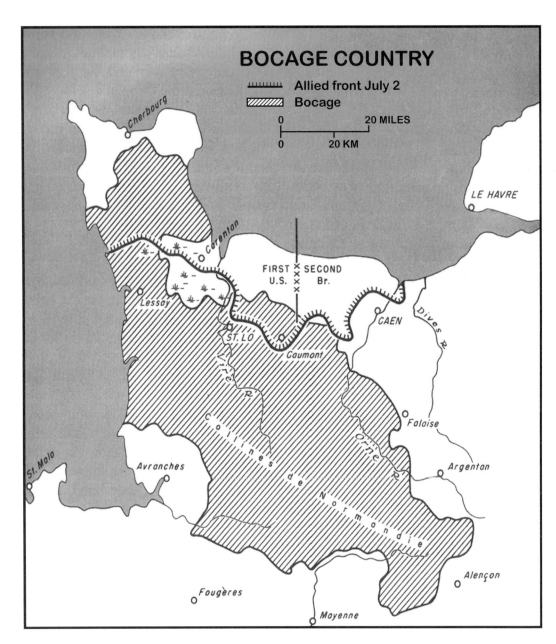

BOCAGE COUNTRY

- ⊥⊥⊥⊥⊥ Allied front July 2
- ▨▨▨ Bocage

0   20 MILES
0   20 KM

Cherbourg

LE HAVRE

Carentan

FIRST ×× SECOND
U.S. ×× Br.

Lessay

CAEN

Dives R.

ST. LO

Caumont

Vire R.

Collines de Normandie

Orne R.

Falaise

St. Malo

Avranches

Argentan

Fougères

Alençon

Mayenne

The bocage dominates the countryside of three French départements: most of Manche, and parts of Calvados and Orne.

Chapter One

The Bocage

The bocage country of France extends from the Cotentin Peninsula in a wide swathe southeast almost as far as Falaise and Alençon. Today the roads are metalled and many of the thick hedges have disappeared, obliterated by modern farming techniques and increased industrialisation. In 1944, with fewer roads and many more farm tracks, the countryside was characterised by small fields surrounded with high dense hedges and liberally sprinkled with copses. It presented a difficult, claustrophobic battlefield to Allied forces whose martial strongpoints were based around mobility and movement. Constrained by the challenging terrain, and with the balance of power firmly weighted towards the defenders, progress was slow and Allied casualty rates appalling.

While this countryside stretches well east and south of Saint-Lô, impeding British attempts to work their way around the western edges of Caen, in the initial weeks after D-Day it was the US First Army that had to fight southwards through the bocage, This so-called Battle of the Hedgerows was as frustrating for the American forces in Normandy as the battle for Caen was for the British. Harried by their own Press, willed on not only by their nation but the entire free world, it is unsurprising that so much pressure was put on the top commanders—Eisenhower, Montgomery, and Bradley in particular—and all the way down the food chain. Having breached the Atlantic Wall and taken Cherbourg at a gallop, with air superiority over the battlefield and dominance at sea, everyone expected the Allies to advance quickly deep into France.

It was not to be. The German defence was tenacious and had had years to understand and prepare its ground. The weather was atrocious, the worst for many years, so bad in fact that it destroyed one of the Mulberry harbours reducing supply operations substantially and leaving First Army short of artillery ammunition and other essential requirements. Bradley said, 'Weeks of intermittent rain had shrouded the beachhead with a dismal gray cloud cover pinning the air forces to the ground while the enemy dragged up reinforcements.' And then, as discussed, there was the terrain: swamps and flooded rivers initially; hedgerows thereafter.

Three aerial views of the Normandy hedgerows. In the small, densely foliaged fields of the bocage, every hedge might hide a machine gun, every path a minefield, every tree a sniper. Good metalled roads were few and far between, which made transport hubs such as St-Sauveur-le-Vicomte, Carentan, and Saint-Lô vital targets. In the bocage, 'a skilful defending force can cause great delay and heavy losses to an attacking force many times stronger. This because the attacker can't use his firepower effectively and because he can't advance rapidly.' German defenses included heavy MGs to rake the open fields, designated pre-planned mortar target areas, snipers, dugouts using telephone communications to ensure a coordinated defense, booby traps and mines. At a longer distance, 88s, tanks, and artillery picked off anyone unwary enough to show themselves. As the Germans didn't defend every field, the attackers were kept guessing, which sapped mental energy and led to an increase in battle fatigue casualties.

Following page: Men of CCB, 2nd Armored Division in a sunken lane in the bocage around Le Pont Brocard south of Saint-Lô. As Lt-Col (Retd) Hugh F. Foster III put it, 'The men in the combat elements of a rifle company faced a bleak future in which virtually everyone would be killed, wounded, injured, taken prisoner or felled by illness. That the soldiers who served the cause of freedom and fought so nobly for mankind and their comrades knew this dismal reality, yet soldiered on in spite of it is a wonder and a great testament to the character of the American GI of WWII.'

Communications were difficult in the bocage. Radios were unreliable and subject to interception—the Germans were scathing about Allied radio procedures and the information they were able to pick up. Because of this, wire was laid and telephones were often used. German Generalleutnant Albert Praun said, 'The expansion of the beachheads resulted in the transmission of so many radio messages that a fairly clear picture of the enemy situation was speedily obtained. An even greater wealth of information was provided by short-range radio intelligence and divisional combat intelligence.' However, the Germans themselves weren't always brilliant: Panzer Lehr's movement west and counter-attack towards St-Fromond was telegraphed by poor radio discipline.

Life in the front line: resting in a dugout along a hedge line. As in all wooded areas, one of the problems of the bocage was protection from wood splinters caused by airbursts—good reason to cover a trench with tree trunks or use a foxhole. Here, (**Right**) Sgt E. Vandenburg of the US 35th Infantry Division shelters in a German foxhole near Saint-Lô on 23 July 1944.

Above Left: Firepower was critical in the Battle of the Hedgerows. American artillery was a key factor in victory. Here, a camouflaged artillery position near St-Jean-de-Daye.

Left and Above: Rifle grenades immediately improved the infantryman's reach: a hand-thrown grenade has a range of around 30 yards while a rifle grenade can be fired up to over 150 yards. A simple attachment (the M7 launcher), a booster cartridge, the M15 auxiliary sight and a rubber recoil boot enabled an M1 Garand to fire a range of grenades.

Left: The untested American infantrymen left their training areas in England and were plunged into the claustrophobic hedges and ditches of the bocage. Visibility was even worse with the summer growth and the conditions weren't helped by the wettest June/July weather for some years. In the hedgerows, small-scale localized German defense combined fields of interlocking fire from prepared positions, pre-ranged artillery and a high level of MGs to make the going slow and dangerous, nullifying the Allies' advantages of manpower and equipment. But, the attrition was two-sided, and as the German forces were pushed back by the inexorable Allied tide, they were slowly ground down.

Above: The only way to cross open ground in the bocage: at speed and with covering fire. Note the .30-cal LMG carried by the man at right.

Below: The infantryman's closest friend was his entrenching tool. North of Saint-Lô, men of the 175th Infantry Regiment of the 29th Infantry Division dig-in close to a hedge on 15 July.

Above and Below: Extraction of casualties was managed by various vehicles, including specially commissioned jeeps as seen here.

Right: Casualties were high in Normandy, and the main casualties were inevitably front-line infantry. Bradley discusses the problem in *A Soldier's Story*: before D-Day the projected casualty figures for the men in the front line was 70 percent. In reality, the figure in the bocage was nearer 83 percent. At Saint-Lô, 'in 15 days the 30th Division sustained 3,924 battle casualties. ... Because three out of every four of those casualties occurred in a rifle platoon, the rate of loss in those platoons exceeded 90 percent.' The high hedgerows made casualty extraction difficult and often hampered by German snipers. From 10 June casualties were flown from Normandy to hospitals in England. By 31 July, 25,959 American wounded had been air evacuated from France (almost a third of all US casualties).

Omar Nelson Bradley (1893–1981), the 'Soldier's General', was promoted to head First Army, then promoted Brigadier General on the permanent list on 2 June 1944, five days before he first arrived on French soil for a quick inspection on 7 June. On 9 June he left his floating headquarters, USS *Augusta*, and moved to an orchard just behind Pointe du Hoc. He and First Army fought its way off the beaches and took the Cotentin and the important port of Cherbourg, before striking south towards Saint-Lô through the bocage. It was Bradley who put together the plan for Operation Cobra, begun on 25 July, that broke the deadlock and allowed his former commander, Patton, to exploit the hole in the enemy's lines. On 1 August he relinquished control of First Army to General Courtney H. Hodges and took control of all the American forces in theatre: nearly a million men.

Chapter Two

The Opposing Forces

'Hedgerows divided a good part of Normandy into small, impenetrable fields. So, building on this, the German defenders had preset mortar and artillery fire on the hedgerows in front of their strongpoint and laced the area with booby traps, mined obstacles, early-warning devices, and snipers. Therefore, a US Army infantryman rustling a leaf in the hot summer silence could bring sniper fire, the crack of artillery, or the rip of machine gun fire. Each patch of farmland became its own miniature universe of battle.'

James Carafano sums up the military problems concisely. The Battle of the Hedgerows pitted the often green American troops against a prepared defence. But the German commanders knew that they were trying to keep a genie in a bottle: one slip, and it would be out and once out there would be no stopping it. And that's exactly what happened. The US Army spent nearly two months bottled up by a combination of terrain and increasingly stretched German forces, but when Operation Cobra opened a gap, Third Army sped through. Two months later, the Allies were at the Rhine.

Nevertheless, fighting in the bocage took away most of the Allied advantages. Their armies fought best when mobile. American tanks and tank destroyers may not have had the armour or weaponry of the Tigers and Panthers but they had the advantage of numbers, automotive reliability and good engineering. They could travel a long way, quickly and without breaking down. And if they did, American logistics and resupply meant that there were people there to solve the problems.

In the bocage, there were few metalled roads in 1944. Those that existed were dominated by a few key transport nexuses: Carentan, Saint-Lô, Bayeux. Most 'roads' were farm tracks, or ancient sunken paths that became quagmires when it rained. And rain it did in 1944. Bad weather negated the Allies' most effective weapon—airpower—and helped keep First Army bottled up. The deluge also ensured that the marshy areas, flooded rivers and all the other water sources provided serious obstacles.

Another key feature of the Battle of the Hedgerows was the importance of the high ground. Warfare has always had taking the high ground as a major tenet, but in the bocage it was even more important than that—particularly for the Germans whose lack of aerial support included the lack of reconnaissance and spotting aircraft. Small hills they may have been, but Hill 192, the Martinville Ridge and Hill 122, were crucial to the attack on Saint-Lô. From these dominant positions the defenders could not just see more than those below but they could also direct artillery fire on their enemy.

It was, however, in those small fields, each bounded by thick hedges, that the main battles took place. The casualties were appalling, at World War I levels for the infantry on both sides. The German defenders suffered as much or more than the attacking US forces They 'had suffered so severely in regard to personnel and equipment that the incurred losses could not even nearly be replaced. In this connection, it is important to note that almost all the annihilated and seriously mauled German units had been committed against the American invasion army.' (*Fighting the Breakout*)

US First Army Attacking forces on 6 June (D-Day)

V Corps (Maj-Gen Leonard Gerow)
1st Infantry Division: Maj-Gen Clarence R. Huebner; **29th Infantry Division:** Maj-Gen Charles H. Gerhardt; **2nd Infantry Division:** Maj-Gen Walter M. Robertson; **Provisional Ranger Group:** Lt-Col James E. Rudder; **Special Engineer Task Force:** Col John T. O'Neil; **3rd Armored Group:** Col Severan D. McLaughlin; **Provisional Engineer Special Brigade Group:** Brig-Gen William M. Hoge

16th RCT of 1st Infantry Division	**116th RCT of 29th Infantry Division**	**Follow up units**
16th Infantry Regiment	116th Infantry Regiment	18th RCT of 1st Infantry Division
741st Tank Battalion	C Coy, 2nd Ranger Battalion	18th Infantry Regiment
Special Engineer Task Force	5th Ranger Battalion	745th Tank Battalion
7th Field Artillery Battalion	743rd Tank Battalion	32nd and 5th Field Artillery
62nd Armd Field Artillery Battalion	Special Engineer Task Force	Battalions
197th AAA Battalion	111th Field Artillery Battalion	5th Engineer Special Brigade
1st Engineer Battalion	58th Armd Field Artillery Battalion	
5th Engineer Special Brigade	4677th AAA Battalion	115th RCT of 29th Infantry
20th Engineer Combat Battalion	121st Engineer Battalion	Division
81st Chemical Warfare	6th Engineer Special Brigade	115th Infantry Regiment
Battalion (mortars)	112th Engineer Combat Battalion	110th Field Artillery Battalion
	81st CW Battalion	
	461st Amphibious Truck Coy	26th RCT of 1st Infantry Division
		26th Infantry Regiment
		33rd Field Artillery Battalion

Forces used in the Battle of the Hedgerows:

V Corps (Maj-Gen Leonard Gerow)
2nd Infantry Division (Maj-Gen Walter M. Robinson)
9th, 23rd and 38th Infantry Regiments; 2nd Recon Troop; 2nd ECB; 12th Field Artillery Battalion (155mm howitzers); 15th, 37th and 38th Field Artillery Battalions (105mm howitzers); 741st Tank Battalion attached

5th Infantry Division (Maj-Gen. S. Leroy Irwin)
2nd, 10th and 11th Infantry Regiments; 5th Recon Troop; 7th ECB; 21st Field Artillery Battalion (155mm howitzers); 19th, 46th and 50th Field Artillery Battalions (105mm howitzers); 735th Tank Battalion and 818th TD Bn (SP) attached

28th Infantry Division (Maj-Gen Lloyd D. Brown until 14 August)
109th, 110th and 112th Infantry Regiments; 28th Recon Troop; 103rd ECB; 108th Field Artillery Battalion (155mm howitzers); 107th, 109th and 229th Field Artillery Battalions (105mm howitzers); 744th Tank Battalion and 630th TD Bn (SP) attached

VII Corps (Maj-Gen J. Lawton Collins)
1st Infantry Division (Maj-Gen Clarence R. Huebner)
16th, 18th and 26th Infantry Regiments; 1st Recon Troop; 1st ECB; 5th Field Artillery Battalion (155mm howitzers); 7th, 32nd and 33rd Field Artillery Battalions (105mm howitzers)

4th Infantry Division (Maj-Gen Raymond O. Barton)
8th, 12th and 22nd Infantry Regiments; 4th Recon Troop; 20th Field Artillery Battalion (155mm howitzers); 29th, 42nd and 44th Field Artillery Battalions (105mm howitzers); 746th Tank Battalion and 899th TD Bn (SP) attached

9th Infantry Division (Maj-Gen Manton S. Eddy)
139th, 47th and 60th Infantry Regiments; 9th Recon Troop; 15th ECB; 34th Field Artillery Battalion (155mm howitzers); 26th, 60th and 84th Field Artillery Battalions (105mm howitzers); 703rd TD Bn (SP) attached

30th Infantry Division (Maj-Gen Leland S. Hobbs)
117th, 119th and 120th Infantry Regiments; 30th Recon Troop; 105th ECB; 113th Field Artillery Battalion (155mm howitzers); 118th, 197th and 230th Field Artillery Battalions (105mm howitzers); 823rd TD Bn (SP) attached

2nd Armored Division (Maj-Gen Edward H. Brooks)
32nd and 33rd Armored Regiments; 36th Armored Infantry Regiment; 83rd Armored Recon Battalion; 23rd Armored Engineer Battalion; 54th, 67th and 391st Armored Field Artillery Battalions (105mm howitzers)

3rd Armored Division (Maj-Gen Maurice Rose)
66th and 67th Armored Regiments; 41st Armored Infantry Regiment; 82nd Armored Recon Battalion; 17th Armored Engineer Battalion; 14th, 78th and 92nd Armored Field Artillery Battalions (105mm howitzers)

VIII Corps (Maj-Gen Troy H. Middleton)
8th Infantry Division (Brig-Gen Donald A. Stroh after 12 July)
13th, 28th and 121st Infantry Regiments; 8th Recon Troop; 12th ECB; 28th Field Artillery Battalion (155mm howitzers); 43rd, 45th and 56th Field Artillery Battalions (105mm howitzers); 709th Tank Battalion and 644th TD Bn (SP) attached

79th Infantry Division (Maj-Gen I.T. Wyche)
313th, 314th and 315th Infantry Regiments; 79th Recon Troop; 304th ECB; 312th Field Artillery Battalion (155mm howitzers); 310th, 311th and 904th Field Artillery Battalions (105mm howitzers). Co B, 749th Tank Battalion and 813th TD Bn (SP) attached

83rd Infantry Division (Maj-Gen Robert C. Macon)
329th, 330th and 331st Infantry Regiments; 83th Recon Troop; 308th ECB; 224th Field Artillery Battalion (155mm howitzers); 322nd, 323rd and 908th Field Artillery Battalions (105mm howitzers); Co C, 749th Tank Battalion and 644th TD Bn (SP) attached

90th Infantry Division (Maj-Gen Eugene M. Landrum until 30 July)
357th, 358th and 359th Infantry Regiments; 90th Recon Troop; 315th ECB; 345th Field Artillery Battalion (155mm howitzers); 343rd, 344th and 915th Field Artillery Battalions (105mm howitzers)

4th Armored Division (Maj-Gen John S. Wood)
8th, 35th and 37th Tank Battalions; 10th, 51st and 53rd Armored Infantry Battalions; 25th Cavalry Recon Sqn; 24th Armored Engineer Battalion; 22nd, 66th and 94th Armored Field Artillery Battalions (105mm howitzers)

XIX Corps (Maj-Gen Charles H. Corlett)
29th Infantry Division (Maj-Gen Charles H. Gerhardt)
115th, 116th and 175th Infantry Regiments; 29th Recon Troop; 121st ECB; 227th Field Artillery Battalion (155mm howitzers); 161st, 216th and 219th Field Artillery Battalions (105mm howitzers)

35th Infantry Division (Maj-Gen Paul W. Baade)
134th, 137th and 320th Infantry Regiments; 35th Recon Troop; 60th ECB; 127th Field Artillery Battalion (155mm howitzers); 118th, 197th and 230th Field Artillery Battalions (105mm howitzers); 737th Tank Battalion and 654th and 821st TD Bn (SP) attached

Above: Tankers prepare their night's bivouac.

Below: This photograph gives a good idea of how the hedgerows impeded tankers' vision and made life easier for the defender.

Above, Right Above and Below: Italy saw the first combat use of the Sherman Bulldozer and the lessons learned there ensured that they were in high demand after D-Day. Unfortunately, in spite of Eisenhower's personal interest, too few were manufactured. The dozer Sherman was probably the best method of breaking through the bocage hedgerows (seen here). These VVSS Shermans are equipped with an M1 blade; the M1A1 equipped the slightly wider HVSS Shermans.

Left: Stuart equipped with a Culin cutter. Some M5s were equipped with dozer blades. They had their turrets removed and saw action in the Pacific.

Left: Sgt Curtis G. Culin III (1915–1963) of the 102nd Cavalry Recon Squadron, in his M5A1 on 29 July. A New Yorker, he lost a leg in the Hürtgen Forest battles in November.

Below Left: Welder-mechanics of the 705th Ordnance Coy torch the hedgehogs recovered from the beaches to make Culin hedgerow cutters.

Above and Below: During the battles in the hedgerows a number of different hedge-cutting devices were used, but the one that stuck was the work of Sgt Curtis G. Culin III. Bradley tells the tale in *A Soldier's Story*. Invited to 2nd Division by Lt-Gen Leonard T. Gerow to see 'something that will knock your eyes out,' he witnessed a light tank and a Sherman breaking through a hedgerow thanks to 'four tusk-like prongs.' Immediately recognising the potential, Bradley ordered his ordnance officer, Lt-Col John B. Medaris (1902–1990; later Maj Gen), to duplicate these on a large scale. Within a week, three out of every five tanks had one. Culin received the Legion of Merit. In fact, possibly too much has been made of the 'Rhino' tanks. In *After D-Day* James Carafano labels the importance placed on them by postwar writers a myth, and Stephen Zaloga says that in many interviews tank crew expressed mixed views about their efficacy. What was needed were more tank dozers because there were only 40 when Cobra started.

Left: Different styles of hedgerow cutter exhibited on an M4 in Brittany and an M5 passing through St-Amand, south of Saint-Lô.

Above: There were 20 US TD battalions in Normandy, 15 equipped with M10s (as here) and five with M18 Hellcats.

Artillery was a huge factor on the Normandy battlefield and the Germans had less of it than the Allies. Added to the quantity, proximity to the shoreline ensured that the mighty weapons of the Allied naval vessels were able to support the ground forces. US and British artillery was the match for anything the Germans had: excellent weapons, communications equipment, and fire control systems. Observers or artillery officers could be found in or near the front lines, calling down artillery barrages as required—for example what the British called the 'stonk' and the US Army the 'time-on-target' concentration. This focused fire from several battalions onto a selected target. The photo (**Below**) shows a 155mm howitzer of the 20th FA Battalion from 4th Infantry Division. Each division had a battalion of medium artillery—155mm howitzers.

Right: An American 57mm antitank gun in action near Saint–Lô. A copy of the British 6-pdr, it was widely used in US infantry divisions.

Below Right: In US Army service, the Bofors 40mm Automatic Gun M1 fired three variants of the British Mk. II HE shell but could also fire the M81A1 armour-piercing round. The Anti-Aircraft Artillery auto-weapons battalion was organised around four batteries for a total of 32 guns.

Above: 81mm (3.2-inch) mortar near Saint-Lô. The battalion heavy weapons company included an 81mm mortar platoon of six tubes. A powerful weapon, the 81mm could lob a 15lb HE round to a range of over 3,000 yards.

Above Right: The crew lifts the camouflage net from a US M2 4.2-inch mortar. Rifled, this was a sizeable weapon that could drop an 8-pound warhead some 4,000 yards. It was employed in chemical mortar battalions with four companies each of three four-tube platoons.

Right: 4.2-inch ammunition was rifled and did not have fins.

Above Left: AAA weapons in the ground role—four Browning M2HB .50s lay down a lot of suppressing fire. The M45 Quadmount entered service in 1943 either as a towed trailer or on an M16 halftrack. The 'meat chopper' proved effective in the bocage.

Left: The only problem with the water-cooled .30-cal Browning M1917 machine gun was its weight: the gun, tripod, water and ammo together weighed 103lb.

Above: In the bocage southwest of Saint-Lô, near St-Ouen-des-Besaces, a 60mm M2 mortar is prepared for action. The rounds are M49A2 HE shells that had a range of 200 to 2,000 yards (the latter when assisted by boosting charges).

Above: Laying down sufficient supporting machine-gun fire was an essential part of bocage fighting. The main US MGs were at squad level, the .30-cal Browning Automatic Rifle—the BAR. One man fired it, but there was an assistant gunner and an ammunition man. Companies could provide their platoons with heavier firepower from their weapons platoon, which had two Browning .30-cal MGs (the M1919 air-cooled, as here) or heavy, water-cooled M1917s (see page 40).

Above and Left: Rifle companies had five three-man antitank rocket teams that were attached to platoons as necessary. Introduced in 1942, the US bazookas were not as effective as the Panzerschreck against AFVs particularly when head on, but nevertheless accounted for a number of enemy tanks from the side and rear. Above, at right, swabbing out an M1A1 bazooka. This was an improved version of the M1. Introduced in 1943, the M1A1 fired M6A1 HEAT rounds that could penetrate around three inches of armour.

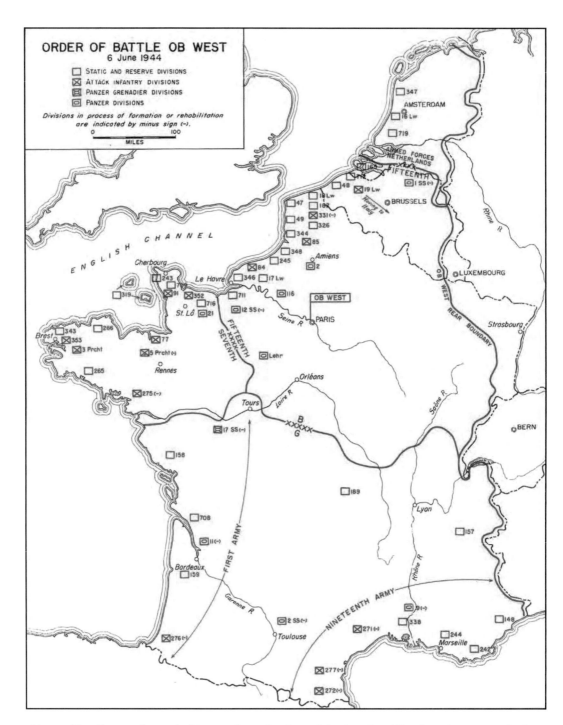

Above: The German forces in Normandy at the time of the invasion. The American sector had been beefed up by the arrival of 352nd Infanterie-Division, among whose ranks were a number of Eastern Front veterans as well as conscripts and Ost volunteers.

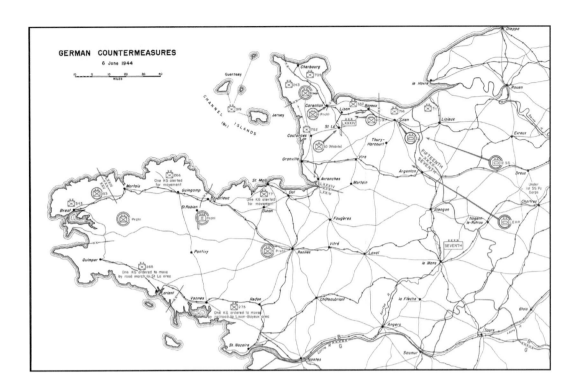

GERMAN COUNTERMEASURES
6 June 1944

 Static division

 Corps reserve

 Army reserve

 Army group and reserve

 OKW reserve

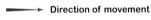

→ Direction of movement

KG   Kampfgruppe

────── Main railroads

────── Highways

Above: German countermeasures to the invasion included moving their armour reserves to the front. However, most of this was tied down by the British attacks around Caen: so much so that at no stage did US forces come into contact with the heavy Panzer battalions—mainly Tiger Is and latterly some Tiger IIs—that proved so effective in the defence of Caen. The bocage was not great country for Tigers: they were at their most effective when able to use the long-range hitting power of their 88mm main gun. The main threat to US forces were the StuG assault guns, the ubiquitous PzKpfw IVs and the PzKpfw V Panthers. The Germans rushed their reserves to Normandy once the impact of the invasion was felt, but crucially left a large number of troops in the Pas-de-Calais. Deceived by Operation Fortitude, the German High Command could have dealt the invasion forces much harsher treatment had they reacted faster. As it was the reinforcements came to the battlefield piecemeal, harried by Allied air forces and immediately thrown into the defence as they arrived. No significant counterattack was launched but they were able to achieve parity. This equality of forces, linked to the defendable terrain, enabled the Germans to stave off the continual Allied thrusts until the end of July. When Operation Cobra opened the gap the German position deflated like a punctured balloon.

192520

Above Left: German armour wasn't all Tigers, in spite of what the Allied infantry reported. The PzKpfw IV, with nearly 9,000 units built, was far and away the most numerous of the German tanks, and amongst the best. Designed by Krupp to a specification raised in 1934, it proved the perfect platform for upgrading and upgunning. Around 1,000 of the 'short' version were built, mainly Ausf. E and F, and used for infantry support. The main production run centred around the Ausf. G, H and J, which totalled 7,500 units with the long 75mm KwK 40 L/48 gun, and many with side skirts (*Schürzen*) for protection against bazooka and other HESH rounds. Here, on the way to Vire, PzKpfw IV No 802 of 8./Pz-Regt 4 of 2nd Pz Div was knocked out during the liberation of Pont-Farcy by 35th Inf Div on 2 August.

Left: The heavier PzKpfw V Panther was an extremely good tank, with an excellent gun and good frontal armour. There weren't many in Normandy initially, but by the end of July there were just over 400. Effective in tank country, in the bocage the Panther was not at its best and US antitank forces—especially bazooka teams and artillery—picked them off. The M10 that disposed of this Panther can be seen in the field behind.

Above: Like the US tank destroyers, the Marder III had an open-topped turret and was, therefore, vulnerable to grenades and airbursts. Lightly armed, it mated obsolete tank chassis (mainly the Panzer 38(t)) with the 75mm PaK 40 anti-tank gun. Around 3,500 were built/converted and they saw action until the end of the war.

Above: The German Army had good artillery and its 88mm Flak/antitank weapon is legendary. The PaK 40 75mm was the main German antitank gun—around 20,000 were manufactured— mostly in towed form, but it was also used on tank destroyers such as the Marder series (see the previous page).

Below: The Sturmgeschütz III and IV (depending on chassis) assault guns were built in large numbers (10,000+ and 1,000+ respectively). Armed initially with 75mm StuK 37 L/24 guns, as they became more used as tank destroyers they were upgunned to the 75mm StuK 40 L/48.

Above Right: The Germans placed a high reliance on mortars. The Juno Centre quotes the British official historian, L.F. Ellis, 'In the latter stages of the war German interest in conventional field and medium artillery seems to have been on the wane. Instead they were setting more store by mortars and Nebelwerfer, of which they had large numbers in Normandy.' This is the standard German infantry mortar, the 80mm Granatwerfer 34 (GrW 34).

Below Right: The MG42 excelled in the confines of the bocage used either from a bipod or the more substantial tripod shown here. Because of its high rate of fire it required frequent barrel changes—which could be accomplished quickly—and used a great deal of ammunition. This meant that most of the squad men had to carry extra rounds for the machine gun.

Left: The Erbsenmuster (or pea-dot) 1944 camouflage clothing was used exclusively by the Waffen-SS.

Above: The 15cm Nebelwerfer 41 was the main version of the feared 'Moaning Minnie'. Most were opposite the British and Canadian forces.

Below: In the bocage First Army ground down their opponents in a grim war of attrition with casualty levels near those of the trench warfare of WW1. Between 6 June and 11 July, in the bocage country around Saint-Lô and leading up to Operation Cobra, the Germans lost over 16,000 men of 243rd and 342nd Divisions; and Panzer Lehr lost over 3,000. In total over 200,000 Germans became PoWs during the Normandy campaign.

Above Left: The Allies called it the 'Schmeisser', but in fact it had nothing to do with him. The MP40 was manufactured in large quantities (over a million) during the war and it proved to be an excellent close-combat weapon.

Left: Antitank ambushes with guns, Panzerfaust or Panzerschreck (illustrated) ensured a continuous attrition of armour and crew—but as tactics evolved the ambushers themselves were attacked by supporting infantry.

Above: Shirt O.D. ... Jackets Field ... Trousers O.D.: the QM Corps was responsible for ensuring soldiers were properly equipped. For the most part, it performed well until the supply lines became over-extended after the Allied victory in France.

After the beating they took on Omaha Beach, 1st and 29th Infantry Divisions pushed south, taking up positions to the northeast of Saint-Lô. 1st Infantry would take no further part in the campaign until after the city fell, but the 29th was heavily involved in the attack. Here, M8s of 29th Recon Squadron of the 29th Division's Task Force Cota are seen on Saint-Lô's Place Sainte-Croix. For the battle of Saint-Lô see Chapter Six.

Chapter Three

Advance from Omaha

Unlike Utah, landing on Omaha was horrific. Initailly, the attackers couldn't get off the beach and were decimated as they arrived. Significantly behind schedule, Bradley 'contemplated the diversion of follow-up forces to Utah and the British beaches.' However, slowly, small groups of men managed to infiltrate the bluffs—generally thanks to landing away from the direct fire of a *Widerstandsnest*, or where the fog of war and smoke from fires helped obscure them from the Germans. Around Les Moulins draw, urged on by Gen. 'Dutch' Cota, the 5th Rangers led the way with small groups of 116th Infantry. Elsewhere, 16th Infantry infiltrated between St.-Laurent and Colleville. Aided by the surviving tanks on the beach and by the supporting fire from destroyers which approached close enough to ground, the deadlock was broken. The battle for the beach moved into the hinterland.

First task was to link with the bridgehead on the Cotentin. In the early hours of 8 June, the Rangers who had landed on Omaha, elements of 116th Infantry Regiment and tanks from the 743rd Tank Battalion reached the Rangers at Pointe du Hoc. Further south, 29th Division pushed westwards, and, aided by naval fire from the British cruiser *Glasgow*, 175th Infantry Regiment and tanks of the 747th Tank Battalion entered Isigny on the 9th. While the town was in flames, the bridge over the Aure was intact, and no organised resistance was met in the town. The way to Carentan was clear from the east, and from the west Carentan itself was taken by 101st Airborne from FJR6 on 12 June. The subsequent German counterattack—the battle of Bloody Gulch—beaten back on 13 June thanks to the timely arrival of CCA/2nd Armored from Omaha.

South of Omaha, 1st and 29th Infantry Divisions pushed the remnants of German 352nd Division in front of them. The fighting was tough but with the arrival of 2nd Armored Division after D+4, American attacks caused the left flank of the division to collapse. On the night of 9–10 June, the 352nd retreated and its withdrawal created a big gap between the remaining defenders: Panzer-Lehr Division to the west and 12th SS-Panzer to the east. 2nd Panzer Division was supposed to fill the gap, but on 10 June it was still in transit and not expected to arrive in strength until 13 June.

1st Infantry surged forward to Caumont-l'Éventé. To its left, 7th Armoured Division hurried forward too. The Germans, in the meantime, sent the Tigers of SS-sPzAbt 101 to plug the gap. The resulting battle at Villers-Bocage is described on pp. 136–139.

At Caumont in late June the war slowed down as bigger events took place elsewhere. 1st Infantry held its position until after the Battle for Saint-Lô.

Above: After the hell of Omaha Beach, V Corps and XIX Corps pushed south into the bocage. After the fall of Isigny 29th Division (XIX Corps) reached Neuilly-la-Forêt, the command post of Grenadier-Regiment 914 (352. Infanterie-Division), on 9 June. This photo was taken after the village was liberated in front of the church of Notre-Dame of the Assumption. The 56th General Hospital was set up east of Neuilly-la-Forêt, and to the north airfield A-11 was constructed. It was mainly used by 474th Fighter Group, 6 August–5 September.

Above Right: Trévières housed the command post of Grenadier-Regiment 916 (352. Infanterie-Division) and was attacked by 12nd Infantry Division (see following page).

Right: The 115th Infantry Regiment of 29th Division moved south after landing, taking St-Laurent-sur-Mer on the 7th and after heavy fighting reached the Elle River at Ste-Marguerite-d'Elle which was taken during the afternoon of 10 June.
On 11 June the 1st and 2nd battalions were placed in reserve in the village while the 3rd battalion prepared to cross the Elle the next day. (See page 000.)

Trévières was initially attacked by elements of 1st Infantry Division on 8 June. Heavily bombarded from the sea, later that day the 38th Infantry Regiment of the newly landed 2nd Infantry Division took up the battle. Intense fighting saw the village fall to the division with a final attack on 10 June. A few days later, on 15 June, the body of a German soldier of II./Infanterie-Regiment 916 is still lying in Place du Marché (**Above**).

Above: East of Le Molay-Littry, near a shrine, a PzKpfw 35R (f) armed with a 47mm PaK (t) of 3./ Schnelle Abteilung 517 lies abandoned. Schnelle-Brigade 30 was part of Seventh Armee's reserve. It was deployed on 6 June to aid 916 IR (352.ID) between Trévières and Bayeux.

Above Right and Right: All dressed up for liberation, French townspeople of Balleroy watch men of the 7th (L) Field Artillery Bn of the 1st US ID pass. They saw little significant fighting to Caumont.

Above: An interesting event took place on 2 July, when nine German nurses who had been captured in Cherbourg were returned to the German lines. The arrangements were made at Balleroy where a short cease-fire was agreed and the nurses were taken through the lines at Caumont-l'Éventé—with a Press fanfare. Often captured medical personnel were kept to provide medical care to PoWs.

Right: This well-known sequence of photos shows a B-26C of the 323rd BG, 98th BW of the Ninth Air Force above the forest of Balleroy around 7 June. Note the white band on the natural metal tail. The nickname of this group was the 'white tails'.

Left: The 526th Ord Tank Maintenance Co landed on Omaha on 8 June and moved to the Foret de Cerisy on 11 June where they stayed until Saint-Lô fell. Among other things, 'our welders worked all night producing and installing the device on as many tanks as could be equipped with it before the Saint-Lô breakthrough. It was not a sensation but was reasonably successful and undoubtedly helped in solving the hedgerow problem.'

Above: M5A1 *Concrete* of 2nd Armored. The division landed on Omaha on 9–10 June, but had suffered casualties before the landings when an LST hit a mine and lost 31 tanks and 15 other vehicles as well as 66 men. On the beach itself the 29th were badly hit—the 116th Regiment alone had 1,007 casualties including 247 dead. 82nd Recon Bn and other regimental recon companies were sent forwards first towards Caumont to shore up 1st Infantry's exposed flank. CCA was sent to Carentan to help the 101st Airborne. They arrived in the nick of time, halting a German counterattack that threatened to overwhelm the paras. On 19 June 2nd Armored went into reserve, waiting for the rest of its units from the UK and then involvement in Operation Cobra.

Above: St-Paul-du-Vernay was the location of the CP of Grenadier-Regiment 915 (352. Infanterie-Division) and, after it fell on 2 July, 2nd Armored Division.

Above Right: A 2nd Armored Div M5 passes La Tuilerie, a hamlet of Le Tronquay, while the division was in reserve around Balleroy.

Below Right: A 2nd Armored Div Sherman about to be camouflaged at St-Paul-du-Vernay. Although the Allies had air superiority, German bombers did venture over the battlefield and camouflage was essential.

Caumont-l'Éventé was liberated on the morning of 13 June after four days of fighting as 1st Infantry Division clashed with 2nd Panzer Division. The American forces would stay here, at the tip of a salient, until Cherbourg had been taken and the July offensive started—Bradley being loath to expend resources possibly needed for the Cherbourg campaign elsewhere. The boundary between the British and American forces was moved westward and in July the British attacked south from here.

Left: A sandbagged position in Caumont.

Above: Making an ass of themselves? A bit of fun in Caumont.

The expansion from the beaches by XIX and V Corps saw 29th Division take St-Clair-sur-l'Elle and 2nd Infantry Division take Bérigny, St-Georges-d'Elle and St-Germain-d'Elle. The hedgerow battles were extremely costly: 29th Div sustained 547 casualties 10–11 June. *GI Stories'* pamphlet on 2nd Infantry talks of one company losing 17 men on one day and 15 the next. Rifle companies would see 90 percent attrition during the campaign. Often it was the artillery that saved the day, with over 6,000 rounds fired by US gunners around St-Clair-sur-l'Elle during the battle.

Above Left and Right: Bérigny, artillery liaison for 2nd Infantry Division.

Below: An aerial view of St-Claire-sur-l'Elle. Although the Elle river is small by any standards, it was a serious obstacle with artillery and machine guns ranged around the area. Held on 12 June, Gerhardt pushed the division onwards, and 13 June saw the village taken. The attrition was substantial on both the US forces and on German 352nd Division. The German line was bolstered by the arrival of the extremely well-armed and motivated 3rd Fallschirmjäger Division.

Above Right: On 2 July Eisenhower (in cap) and Bradley visited 29th Division's HQ and were met by the division's band and most of the regimental and battalion COs. At left 'Cowboy Pete' Corlett, CG of XIX Corps, which included 2nd and 3rd Armored and 29th and 30th Infantry divisions.

Below Right: 3rd Armored arrived over Omaha at the end of June. They were 'blooded' in the bocage. Here, 3/32nd Armored Regiment comes to grips with the hedgerows

4th Infantry Division parades in the courtyard of the Hotel Atlantique in Cherbourg, on 29 June 1944. The division had been in continuous action from 6 to 28 June, when the last resistance around Cherbourg ended. During this period, the division sustained over 5,450 casualties with over 800 men killed.

Chapter Four

The Cotentin

Uppermost in the Allies' thoughts was the capture of a major port. The obvious candidate, and a key part of the invasion strategy, was Cherbourg. At the top of the Cotentin Peninsula, Cherbourg was the perfect port to sustain the Allies' attacks in Normandy and Brittany. The Germans realised this. Hitler designated it a *Festung,* and ordered it must be held to the last man. There was a sizeable garrison, numerous defending batteries, including railway guns, and many coastal strongpoints.

Having blown away the opposition in front of the Utah beaches, Bradley first ensured his beachheads at Utah and Omaha were joined. This was achieved by 15 June when Carentan fell to the 101st Airborne. The German defenders, the tough Fallschirmjäger-Regiment 6, mounted a strong defence and, following the town's loss, a quick counterattack in conjunction with elements of SS-Panzergrenadier-Regiment 37 and SS-Panzer-Bataillon 17. 101st Airborne held, but only thanks to the arrival of CCA, 2nd Armored Division, whose timely aid was as a result of an ULTRA warning.

Next, Bradley sealed off the Cotentin Peninsula, with 'Lightning Joe' Collins' VII Corps taking the lead. Aided by 505th PIR and 325th GIR of 82nd Airborne, the American forces attacked westwards taking St-Sauveur-le-Vicomte on 16 June. The defenders were what was left of German 91st Airlanding Division and the newly arrived 77th Infantry Division, the latter giving US 90th Infantry Division such a hard time that it led to the removal of the 90th CG, Brig-Gen Jay W. MacKelvie and its replacement in the line by the 9th Infantry Division. By 18 June, with 9th Infantry's 47th and 60th Infantry Regiments to the fore, First Army reached Barneville-sur-Mer and the defenders of Cherbourg were cut off.

Those defenders were Kampfgruppe von Schlieben, CG of 709th Division, whose force fell back on Cherbourg to regroup. The other German troops in the Cotentin —KG Hellmich—and all mobile artillery were sent south so that they wouldn't be trapped by the American advance. Unfortunately for them, the decision to disengage KG Hellmich came too late and only around 1,500 men escaped.

The attack towards Cherbourg itself was prosecuted with surprising speed considering the bocage terrain. Since D-Day there had been hard fighting on the north flank of VII Corps as 4th Infantry Division and 82nd Airborne's 505th PIR, fought to take the ridge line Quinéville–Montebourg–le Ham from the coast to the Merderet

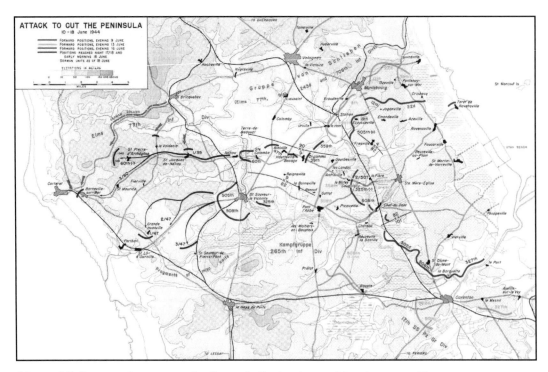

Above: VII Corps strikes across the Cotentin Peninsula, reaching the sea at Carteret.

Above Right: Aerial view of St-Sauveur-le-Vicomte. A Bailey bridge crosses the Douve in the foreground. Note Rommel's asparagus in the fields to prevent glider landings. An important crossroads, St-Sauveur was taken by US 82nd Airborne on 16 June after hard fighting in the bocage. Taking the town opened the way to splitting the Cotentin Peninsula and isolating Cherbourg.

Right: Men of 2/505th PIR, 82nd Airborne with their commander, Lt-Col Benjamin Vandervoort (with the crutch, the result of breaking his ankle on the D-Day drop). Bottom right war photographer Robert Capa crouches changing the film of his camera on 16 June.

River. The Germans held the high ground and had fortified the area making maximum use of the terrain, with strongpoints at Azeville, Crisbecq, Ozeville, and along the beach as far as Quinéville. Taking the battery of Azeville on 9 June opened the way to Quinéville and then on to Montebourg.

On 19 June, Collins sent 9th Infantry up the west side of the peninsula, 79th up the middle and 4th up the east side. Bradley protected his back by putting Troy Middleton's VIII Corps across the neck: the 82nd and 101st Airborne and the 90th Infantry. By the 21st Collins was ready to assault Cherbourg. By the 27th all resistance was over. Cherbourg had fallen but at real cost: 22,119 US casualties including 2,811 dead. On top of this, the port had been effectively destroyed and it would take some time before it could be brought back into use.

Above: Aid station at Étienville on the road to St-Sauveur where the 508th PIR was held in reserve.

Below: St-Sauveur was badly damaged by bombing and artillery, as were the defenders, 91st Airlanding Division. The anti-tank gun is an M1 57mm—a British 6pdr on a narrow carriage designed for airborne use. The soldier carries an M2 bipod for a .30-cal MG.

A US company command conference on the bonnet of a Citroën in St-Saveur. The weapon is a BAR with a bipod attached.

Above: There were V1 sites all over the Cotentin Peninsula, including at Valognes and Bricquebec—the latter shown here. It had good railway connections that were heavily camouflaged, although the Allies had still bombed many of them. The US Army occupied the site and established an important storage centre there.

Below: 2nd Bn, 39th Regiment, 9th Infantry Division liberated Bricquebec on 19 June. This is the scene on 21 June in the Place Sainte-Anne showing the town had suffered less than Valognes and Montebourg. The Germans, now cut off to the south, fled the town heading north.

Right, Above and Below: Aerial views of the town. Note the motte and bailey of the château de Bricquebec, a 13th-century eleven-sided keep standing on a 50-foot motte.

US troops first advanced towards Montebourg from Sainte-Mère-Église on 7 June, but were blocked by elements of 91. and 709. Infanterie-Divisions. By 10 June 4th Infantry Division's 12th Infantry Regiment was close to the town, but was halted by a counterattack that was only broken up by Allied artillery from land and sea. The 4th Infantry offensive to take the town was launched on the 19th supported by Squadron B of 70th Tank Battalion. The Germans finally withdrew north to avoid encirclement and Montebourg—or what was left of it—was liberated on 20 June.

Above Left and Left: Valognes was also badly damaged during the fighting. It was the HQ of Generalleutnant Karl-Wilhelm von Schlieben, CG of German 709th Infantry Division, who became commander of Festung Cherbourg on 23 June. The Germans withdrew from Valognes on 19 June as they retreated to Cherbourg but not before the beautiful medieval town had been flattened—the centre in a bombing raid of 8 and 21 June. This is the Place Vicq d'Azir and the wrecked St-Malo collegiate church which was rebuilt in 1963–67.

Above: Aerial bombardment on hardened concrete shelters often left the personnel within unfit to fight. This R618 bunker was part of WN544—a communication centre for 709. Infanterie-Division.

Right: Organisation Todt had a labour camp in Valognes in which German gypsies were incarcerated along with Jews, homosexuals and political prisoners.

Above: Carteret from the air. On 18 June at 05:00, an armoured column of 9th Inf Div made up of 3rd Bn 60th Inf Regt and tanks of 746th Tk Bn and 899th TD Bn entered the town. The Cotentin Peninsula was now cut off.

Below: 'Lightning Joe' Collins (1896–1987) commanded 25th Inf Div against the Japanese on Guadalcanal and on New Georgia in 1942–43. Eisenhower made him commander of VII Corps in the ETO. Collins arrived in France on D+1, his first mission to cut off the northern Cotentin Peninsula by advancing to the west coast. VII Corps reached Barneville-Carteret on 18 June and then advanced north taking Cherbourg on 27 June. Here Collins (at left) and Capt Kirkpatrick of 79th Inf Div talk on the ramparts of the Fort du Roule, Cherbourg, on 27 June.

Above: StP111 on the Atlantic Wall was St-Vaast-la-Hougue, which had a 667 bunker for a 50mm protecting the harbour entrance and a large bunker that used the Fishermen's church as protection from bombardment There were also various MG posts on the breakwater leading to StP110 La Hougue.

Below: German soldiers in the Ravenoville area surrender on 9 June. There were 47,000 German surrenders in June, 36,000 in July, and around 200,000 during the Normandy campaign as a whole.

Above Left: The attack on Cherbourg started on 22 June. There was heavy fighting, some of the worst on 26 June, when the 22nd Inf Regt of 4th Inf Div attacked Maupertus airfield. They later headed north to take Batterie Hamburg, one of the huge batteries that protected Cherbourg. With the city surrounded, the sizeable garrison—21,000 men commanded by Gen Karl-Wilhelm von Schlieben—was ordered by Hitler to mount a defence to the last man. In fact, after British No. 30 Commando took Octeville, US 79th Infantry Division captured Fort du Roule (high ground at left of this photo), which dominated the city and its defences, on 26 June, and the game was almost up. The garrison held out for two more days, but von Schlieben's troops were 'exhausted in body and spirit, that the port garrison was over-age, untrained, and suffering from "bunker paralysis", and that the leaderless remnants of the 243rd and 77th Divisions were more of a burden than a support.' By the 30th it was all over.

Left: An M4 enters the ruins of Cherbourg.

Above: An iconic image. German prisoners head south from Cherbourg, probably for a camp in Pont à la Vieille on the road to Valognes, some 10 miles away.

Above Left: Cherbourg was not just damaged by bombardment and fighting but also by design. von Schlieben's men fought long enough to allow Konteradmiral Wilhelm Hennecke to disable Cherbourg's port facilities effectively. In *Cross-Channel Attack*, Col. Alvin G. Viney, (who prepared the original engineer plan for port rehabilitation) wrote: 'The demolition of the port of Cherbourg is a masterful job, beyond a doubt the most complete, intensive, and best-planned demolition in history'. Hennecke was awarded the Knight's Cross by Hitler for this.

Left: The Allies took some time to get the facility into shape, the first cargo transiting the port on 16 July, but in August 260,000 long tons came through Cherbourg. On 4 November 19,995 tons of cargo was discharged through Cherbourg including these tanks. In the foreground an M4A3E2 'Jumbo'.

Above: Order in Cherbourg. The MP has acquired a German Kettenkrad. The SdKfz 2 was originally designed to be air-portable and act as a gun tractor. Nearly 9,000 were built 1940–45.

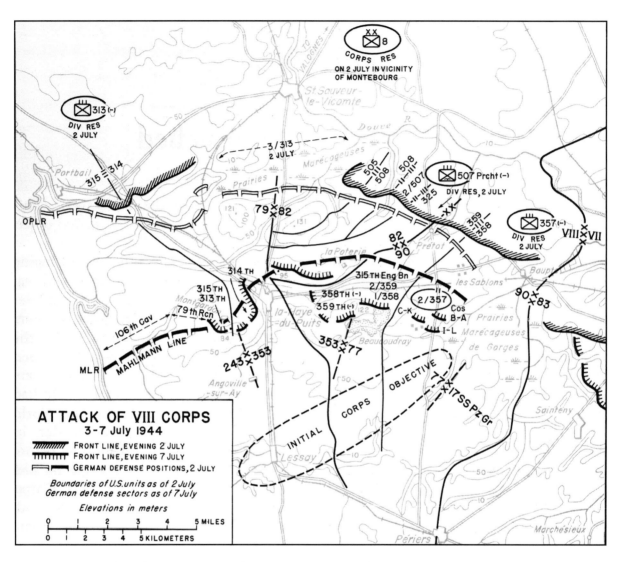

ATTACK OF VIII CORPS
3-7 July 1944

////// FRONT LINE, EVENING 2 JULY
ппппп FRONT LINE, EVENING 7 JULY
⊏⊐⊏⊐ GERMAN DEFENSE POSITIONS, 2 JULY

Boundaries of U.S. units as of 2 July
German defense sectors as of 7 July

Elevations in meters

0 1 2 3 4 5 MILES
0 1 2 3 4 5 KILOMETERS

The first of the major thrusts by First Army, the VIII Corps offensive was prosecuted by 79th, 90th and 82nd Airborne divisions—the latter's last operation before returning to the UK. It was accounted a failure by Martin Blumenson and 90th Division in particular suffered heavily with 2,000 casualties during an advance of only four miles in five days. However, the attack had forced LXXXIV Korps to commit its reserve, Seventh Armee to commit elements of its reserve and OKW to commit the Fallschirmjäger.

Chapter Five

The July Offensive

VIII Corps Attacks

With the Cotentin severed, and VII Corps attacking north toward Cherbourg, Troy Middleton's new VIII Corps became operational on 15 June. The VIII Corps *After Action Report* describes its mission, 'During the period 15–30 June, 1944, the VIII Corps gradually expanded the line across the Cotentin Peninsula from Carentan to Port Bail on the West Coast, with the mission of protecting the southern flank of the VII Corps, while the latter advanced north and captured Cherbourg. The extension of the VIII Corps line was accomplished by the successive acquisition of the 101st Airborne Division, the 82nd Airborne Division, and the 90th and 79th Infantry Divisions. These divisions were disposed generally along the areas inundated by the Germans who, in the preparations of their defenses against the Allied landings, opened the locks of the Douve, Merderet and Taute rivers and permitted the sea to flood the river basins. Small bridgeheads across the inundated areas were established to facilitate the jump-off for an attack south, which was scheduled for the first day of July.'

Hampered by restrictions on ammunition caused by the loss of the US Mulberry harbour to the great storm of 19 June, Middleton's attack finally started down the Coutances road on 3 July, with VII Corps moving south to take over part of the frontage—Collins would be attacking through the marshes south of Carentan. Gen. Matthew Ridgway agreed to have the 82nd spearhead the VIII Corps attack south toward La Haye-du-Puits. Paratroop and glider companies down to less than half-strength led the way for the new, unblooded divisions—and did so in style. The Germans, the 79th Division report outlined, 'with their masterful technique of Hedgerow defensive tactics, stubbornly resisted the advance of the infantry divisions, and the forward movement was measured by the number of fields or orchards taken. ...The only division to attain its first day's objective was the 82nd Airborne. ...The courage and fighting ability of these troops may well stand as a distinguished example to all soldiers.'

Outstripping its flanking units, the 82nd took the high ground in front of La Haye-du-Puits which fell soon after to 79th Division, on 9 July—but not before the 79th had to withstand a strong counterattack, sustaining substantial casualties. The VIII Corps' attack was called off five days later on 14 July. As Bradley said, 'In 12 days he [Middleton] had advanced only 12,000 yards through minefields and against heavy resistance ... it was obvious that the Coutances–Saint-Lô line had become too costly an objective.'

Left: A change of clothing makes all the difference if you've been fighting for days in the rain and mud.

Below: Infantry–tank tactics were the key to success in the bocage, as 90th Division found. Photo dated 7 July as the division advanced on St-Jores.

Right: Prétot-Sainte-Suzanne was liberated on 7 July as 90th Infantry advanced south towards St-Jores. 359th Infantry Regiment suffered heavy casualties.

Above: On 20 July, an MP directs traffic as jeeps and a GMC truck cross Place de l'Eglise in La Haye-du-Puits. The church of Saint John lost one of its spires during the fighting—it has never been replaced. It faces onto what today is named Place Patton.

Right: Aerial views of La Haye-du-Puits. The marshalling yard outside the town was badly bombed on 7 June.

Above: Heading north on rue de Barneville on 4 July. The first man is carrying an 81mm mortar. As the 79th moved out of the line, VIII Corps attacked toward Lessay.

Above Right: Place Ducloux (now Place du Général de Gaulle) in La Haye-du-Puits.

Below Right: Near the castle on 14 July, a Sherman M4 (105) enters La Haye-du-Puits. Note the sign to the right: 'Road cleared to hedges' means that the area is cleared of mines sewn by retreating German forces. Mines were deadly in the bocage, and the Germans were particularly good at siting them in places that advancing troops would use tactically.

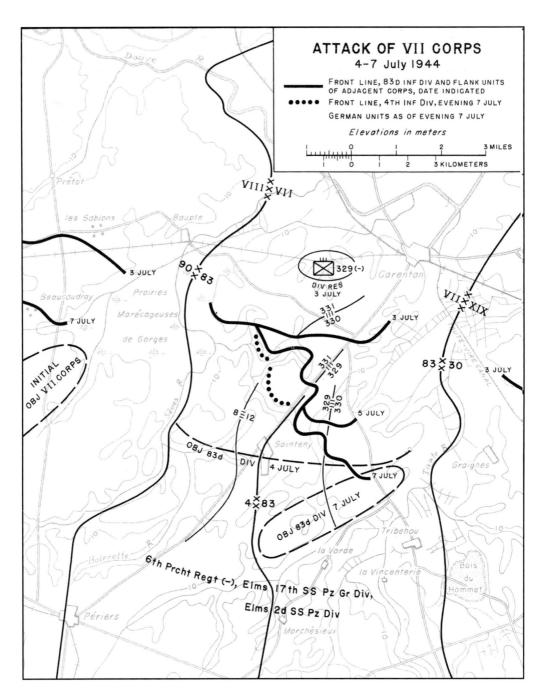

ATTACK OF VII CORPS
4–7 July 1944

—— FRONT LINE, 83D INF DIV AND FLANK UNITS OF ADJACENT CORPS, DATE INDICATED
••••• FRONT LINE, 4TH INF DIV, EVENING 7 JULY
GERMAN UNITS AS OF EVENING 7 JULY

Elevations in meters

Douve R.

Prétot

les Sablions

Baupte

VIII XX VII

90 XX 83

3 JULY

Beaucoudray

Prairies

Marécageuses

de Gorges

7 JULY

INITIAL OBJ VII CORPS

Sèves R.

8 ≡ 12

329 (−)
DIV RES
3 JULY

331 ‖‖ 330

331 ‖ 329

329 ‖ 330

Carentan

VII XX XIX

83 XX 30

3 JULY

3 JULY

5 JULY

OBJ 83d DIV

4 JULY

Sainteny

7 JULY

Graignes

Tauté R.

OBJ 83d DIV

7 JULY

4 XX 83

Tribehou

la Vorde

Holerotte R.

6th Prcht Regt (−), Elms 17th SS Pz Gr Div,

Elms 2d SS Pz Div

Périers

la Vincenterie

Bois du Hommet

Marchésieux

Next to attack was Collins' VII Corps, fresh from its victory at Cherbourg. Between the marshes and the flooded River Taute, first the 83rd and then the 4th infantry divisions pushed hard against a defence that included tough Fallschirmjäger and 2nd SS-Panzer Division Das Reich.

VII Corps Attacks

Following the successful assault on Cherbourg, VII Corps' headquarters immediately moved south to Carentan. Their new sector to the south of the town looked towards what Blumenson calls the 'Carentan–Periers isthmus'. One reason for this appellation is that in 1944 the area was bordered on the west by the swampy marshes of the Prairies Marécageuses de Gorges and on the east by the flooding of the Taute River. It was up this corridor that the Germans counterattacked the 101st Airborne after it had taken Carentan: tipped off by a timely ULTRA warning, Bradley had sent elements of 2nd Armored to help hold the town, the weakest link between the Utah and Omaha lodgements. Now it was to be the scene of a major offensive.

Bradley explains in *A Soldier's Story* that the main reason for this attack was that his breakout plan—codenamed Cobra—starting 10 July was to take place from the jumping off point of the Saint-Lô–Périers main road. But he needed to have taken Périers and got clear of the marshes for that to happen.

There were three significant problems facing the VII Corps. The first was the terrain: the hedgerows hadn't proved a big problem as Collins had chased the Germans up the Cotentin. They were to prove more difficult now as a skilful defence made best use of them. Second, the frontage was only wide enough to have one division in the attack. The plan was for 83rd Infantry Division to advance to Sainteny when Joe Collins hoped he'd be able to widen the line by inserting 4th Infantry Division. The 8th Division would await further developments. The third problem was that the lead division was the 83rd Infantry, which had landed over Omaha Beach on 18 June and hadn't had a chance to put its training into practice. At the end of the first day the 83rd had lost nearly 1,400 men.

The attack started on 4 July, a day after the VIII Corps attack so that the latter could utilise VII Corps' artillery. The Germans—in the form of 17th SS-Panzergrenadier Division with FJR6 attached—were no pushover and with a misty morning and no air cover it was not to be a happy Independence Day. As Blumenson puts it, 'Mishaps plagued the division from the start.' Two days later, Collins threw 4th Infantry into the fray. An experienced division, it had sustained 5,400 casualties since D-Day. Collins thought the problem had been the 83rd: he was wrong. The 4th's attack on 6 July saw nearly 600 casualties as the fighting in the hedgerows intensified.

However, although the US attacks ground to a halt in the bocage, it wasn't just the American forces who were struggling: Seventh Armee was pushed to keep its line intact against the attacks by VIII and VII Corps. Attrition was playing its part. To help, OKW agreed that the 5th Fallschirmjäger Division should leave Brittany and move to the Cotentin from 7 July. That was the day that Maj-Gen Charles H. Corlett's XIX Corps attacked over the Vire.

Above and Below: Communications with family and loved ones was a fundamental requirement in the field. The morale of fighting men while taking awful casualties is boosted by hot food, clean clothes and post. The WW2 Postmaster-General, Frank C. Walker, said in an article in *Army and Navy Journal* 1942, 'officers of the highest rank list mail almost on a level with munitions and food.'

Above Right: Motorcyclists of 2nd Armored Division maintain their Type III 42WLA bikes. Note the HBT one-piece suit on the left, winter combat jackets (tanker jackets) on the two men in the middle and olive drab wool shirt on the right. The bike on the left has a .30-cal ammo can attached to the rear fender.

Below Right: C rations (Field Ration, Type C) were developed in 1938 as pre-cooked tinned food to be used when fresh food wasn't available. Bland and monotonous, a typical ration box (as here) had eight tins of meat and beans; eight tins of meat and vegetable stew; eight tins of meat and vegetable hash; and 24 'Bread unit' cans—containing crackers, sugar and dextrose tablets and a can of beverage mix, coffee or (as indicated here) a powdered synthetic lemon drink. The company identified on the side, Schulze & Burch, was based in Chicago and made the round biscuits.

Above: Men of 4th Infantry Division inspect an ambushed German convoy. In the foreground are the bodies of three German paratroopers of FJR.6; in the background is a VW Schwimmwagen. Photo taken to the west of Sainteny, 16 July.

Right: Soldiers of 329th Infantry Regiment, 83rd Infantry Division recreate the battle of 8–10 July in Sainteny firing a bazooka at a KO'd PzKpfw V Panther of SS-Panzer-Regiment 2 of 2nd SS-Panzer Division Das Reich.

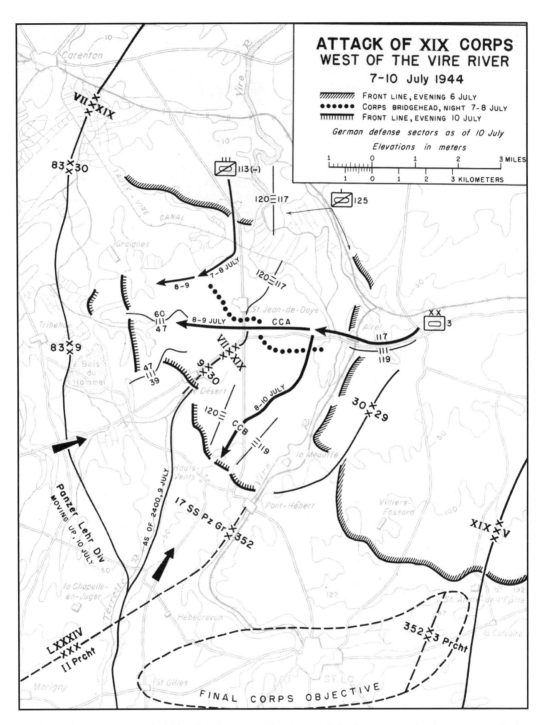

With the first two thrusts held by the German defenders and the bocage causing immense tactical problems and heavy casualties, Bradley started his third corps-level attack on 7 July. XIX Corps attacked across the Vire River and the Vire et Taute Canal.

XIX Corps Attacks

Third time lucky! With the attacks by VIII and VII Corps coming to nothing, the 7 July attack by Maj-Gen Charles H. Corlett's XIX Corps needed to kickstart First Army's push south. Initially, the attack encountered surprisingly light resistance because the over-extended Germans were fighting at La Haye-du-Puits and on the Carentan–Périers isthmus, on the east side of the Vire and the Taute et Vire Canal. As Blumenson says, had the attack taken place a week earlier, it would have been heavily contested. As it was, in spite of the poor weather which negated the anticipated air attacks, the crossing of the Vire was accomplished successfully. Nevertheless, the river crossing by boat was defended and the engineer platoon tasked with getting a footbridge set up lost half its men.

Seizing the river bridge at St-Fromond, 30th Infantry Division took the town and 105th ECB put in the extra bridging necessary to allow 743rd Tank Battalion and, on the 8th, CCA of 3rd Armored, to cross and push on to the strategically important crossroads at St-Jean-de-Daye. By the end of the 8th most of the division and attached tanks were west of the river and the congestion south of St-Daye was building. When CCB/3rd Armored began to cross the bridge at St-Fromond, it just added to the congestion.

The reason for the sudden arrival of 3rd Armored was that the thrust over the Vire had probed a weak point in the German defenses. Once this became obvious, Bradley quickly pushed the division from reserve into the bridgehead. At the same time Rommel and von Kluge sought to nullify the threat, first with 2nd SS-Panzer-Division— at present engaged with the attacks of VIII and VII Corps—and then with Panzer Lehr, at the time heading towards Panzer Group West's reserve.

The US forces were not making the progress that had been hoped. One big reason was that there was massive congestion as the 20-mile long 3rd Armored column tried to advance, while 30th Infantry itself tried to secure the bridgehead with an additional infantry battalion. Enemy artillery destroyed the pontoon that had been set up; the other bridge—a floating treadway—had to be used for returning traffic. In the end it took well into the next morning for CCB to cross. On top of this, General Watson, CG of 3rd Armored, ordered the division to use trails and backroads to advance. It was immediately caught up in the hedgerows with all the problems they engendered.

On the 9th, 2nd SS-Panzer reached Le Dézert but it was forced back by artillery fire—18 battalions of guns were used to do so—but not before it had ambushed B/743rd Tank Bn and knocked out nine tanks. However, just before Panzer Lehr arrived on the scene, Gen Collins persuaded Bradley to commit the unemployed veteran 9th Division (CG: Maj-Gen Manton Eddy) along the east bank of the Taute River. Falling under VII Corps control—as did CCA of 3rd Armored—it had already begun to push south when Panzer Lehr attacked early on the 11th in two columns. The Germans promptly found out exactly how difficult it was to mount an armoured attack in the bocage. Initial confusion aided the penetration, but as morning came, so did the

Above and Above Right: The bridge over the Vire at St-Fromond was taken intact by 30th Infantry Division who had crossed the river earlier. Strengthened by XIX Corps engineers—105th and 247th ECB—it was soon in use. 3rd Armored crossed on 8 July.

Below Right: A contrast between the ruins around the bridge at St-Fromond and a moment of relaxation for two swimsuited men in a canoe, behind two engineers in a boat. The engineers built another bridge alongside the existing bridge to allow two-way traffic, but came under fire while doing so and one company suffered 29 casualties.

antitank teams and soon Panzer Lehr was forced to withdraw, harried by artillery and air strikes. The fighting with 899th TD Bn and 9th Inf Div (north) and 823rd TD Bn and 30th Inf Div (south) had mauled the German division, which went onto the defensive.

30th Infantry CG, Leland Hobbs, replaced CCB's commander, General Bohn, for the lack of success, and Hauts-Vents was taken on 11 July. VII Corps pushed on to the Périers–Saint-Lô highway, but at some cost: by 20 July 30th Division had lost 3,000 men and 9th Division 2,500. Panzer Lehr, however, was down to 40 tanks and TDs and 3,200 combat troops. The stage, however, was set for the attack on Saint-Lô.

Above: Infantrymen of 117th Infantry Regiment supported by two Shermans of the 743rd Tank Battalion in St-Fromond. The closest Sherman is an M4A1 DD with its skirt dismantled.

Below: M10 of B/703rd TD Bn, 3rd Armored, in St-Fromond on 7 July. Under command of Lt-Col Wilbur E. Showalter, the 703rd fought through northern France to the Siegfried Line. It was the first unit to be re-equipped with the M36 90mm GMC.

Above Right: An M5A1 Stuart of the 3rd Armored Div at La Vauterie, a hamlet to the west of St-Fromond. Both were liberated by the 117th Inf. Regt of 30th Inf. Div.

Below Right: Signalmen repair the telephone lines as M5 light tanks pass through a small French village near St-Fromond on 10 July. The men are from 30th Infantry Division and the tank is probably from 2/33rd Tank Regiment, CCB 3rd Armored.

More views of 30th Infantry and 3rd Armored around St-Fromond. The congestion in the area was considerable. Blumenson said, 'General Bohn had quite a task. He had to get 6,000 men in 800 vehicles and 300 trailers, a column over 20 miles long, across a single bridge that was under enemy fire, enter, partially during the hours of darkness, a bridgehead that belonged to another division, and attack a distant objective in strange territory with inexperienced troops.'

Above Left: M5A1.

Below Left: M5 3-inch antitank gun towed by an M3 halftrack

Above: Medium tank of Co C 33rd Armd Regt and M8 armoured car of Co D, 83rd Armd Recon Battalion.

St-Jean-de-Daye was liberated by 30th Infantry Division on 7 July. It proved a useful location for installation of Culin hedgerow cutters once the fighting had eased. Here (**Above Left**) tanks of the 32nd Armored Regiment of 3rd Armored Division in the main square.

Left: Pvt Robert J. Vance from 33rd Armored Regiment, 3rd Armored in St-Jean-de-Daye on his Harley-Davidson WLA. The W identifies its 45cu in side-valve engine; L its high compression; and A the customer, Army. 70,000 were built 1942–45 and it picked up the nickname of 'the Liberator'.

Above: Once liberated, the Allies started to patch together the parts of the infrastructure they needed—in particular the road, rail and transport net. Here, on 23 July the 300th Combat Engineer Battalion reconstructs a railway bridge five miles north of St-Jean-de-Daye.

Below: M10 of 899th TD Bn (9th Inf Div) supports 30th Inf. Div on 11 July during the Panzer Lehr counterattack. The Germans didn't realise that 9th Infantry Division had entered the fray and their counterattack foundered in the bocage. A and C Coys of the 899th TD Bn received a Presidential Unit Citation for their actions.

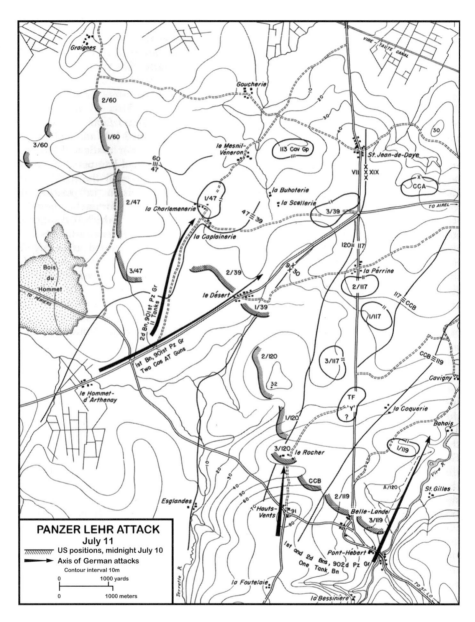

PANZER LEHR ATTACK
July 11

////// US positions, midnight July 10
➤ Axis of German attacks

Contour interval 10m

0   1000 yards

0   1000 meters

The American thrust over the Vire et Taute Canal north of Saint-Lô, prompted Rommel to counterattack, bringing Panzer Lehr from the Caen sector to assist and make use of existing forces—including what remained of Kampfgruppe Heintz and Das Reich. Although Panzer Lehr, commanded by Generalleutnant Bayerlein, was well-equipped and trained, it wasn't at full strength and lacked much of its tank support. First Army shrugged off the attack relegating the reduced German division to a passive defensive role. It would be decimated by the Operation Cobra preparatory bombing.

Above: An M4A1 passes two Das Reich PzKpfw IVs knocked out by men of 117th IR (30th Inf Div). The PzKpfw IVs belonged to Kampfgruppe Wisliceny.

Below: On 14 July near Le Dézert, two M31s recover a burnt-out M4 of 32nd Tank Regt (CCB/3rd Armored) KO'd on 11 July in fighting with Panzer Lehr.

Above: P-47 pilots of 366th Fighter Group based at A-1 St-Pierre-du-Mont check out their victims: 13 Panzer Lehr tanks were claimed by pilots.

Above: Two Panzer Lehr Panther Auf As of I./Pz.Rgt. 6 near Le Dézert, 11 July.
The Germans lost at least 30 tanks during the fighting. The Panther on the left was KO'd by fighter-bombers.

Below: Panther 215 of II./Pz.Rgt.6 is studied by P-47 pilots of the 366th FG and other soldiers,
The 366th FG received the Distinguished Unit Citation for its participation in the failure of the counterattack.

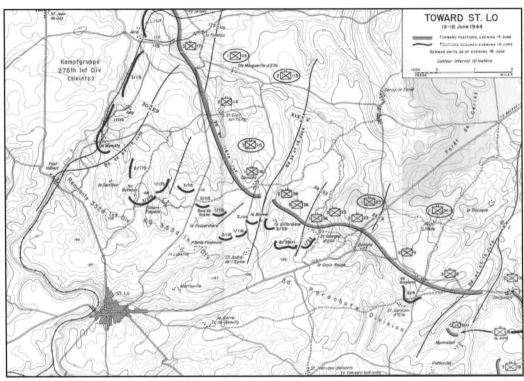

TOWARD ST. LO
14-18 June 1944

Forward positions, evening 14 June
Positions reached evening 18 June
German units as of evening 18 June

Contour interval 10 meters

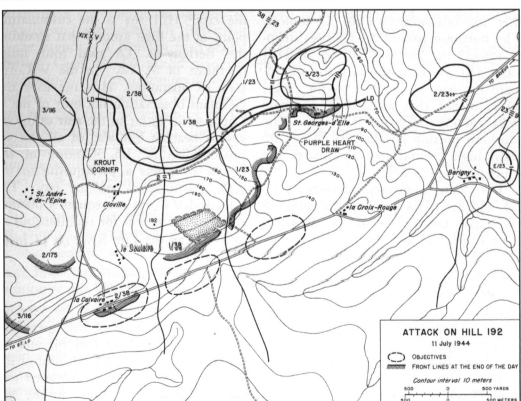

ATTACK ON HILL 192
11 July 1944

OBJECTIVES
FRONT LINES AT THE END OF THE DAY

Contour interval 10 meters

500 YARDS
500 METERS

Chapter Six

The Battle of Saint-Lô

First Army's July offensive had been directed towards Saint-Lô. The city was in many ways Bradley's Caen. He'd expected to capture it nine days after the invasion and, probably wisely, had spurned a fleeting opportunity to take it with 29th Infantry on 13 June. 'I had no intention of pinning down forces at Saint-Lô until Cherbourg was first safely in hand,' he said. However, the strategic importance of Saint-Lô as a transport hub made it an important target—the pre-D-Day bombardment of the railway and power station caused heavy damage that was only made worse by the battle and German artillery after it fell. Additionally, it was crucial for Bradley's breakout operation that Saint-Lô was in American hands. The Germans knew this—they had captured US field orders identifying the importance of Saint-Lô and were determined to hold it.

As First Army continued to fight its way through the hedgerows towards Saint-Lô, XIX Corps had to weather an 11 July counterattack by Panzer Lehr. The German division had already suffered around Caen: now it received short shrift from the Americans. While blunting the counterattack, elements of 30th Infantry and 3rd Armored took Hauts-Vents, high ground that dominated the Pont-Hébert road and river crossing, on 11 July and Pont-Hébert itself on the 14th.

To the east, V Corps—in the form of 2nd Infantry Division—attacked towards Hill 192, the dominant feature overlooking the city, on 12 July. They had tried before in June and at the time sustained over 1,200 casualties. In spite of Seventh Armee's instruction to the defenders (II Fallschirmjäger Korps) to defend at all costs, 2nd Infantry achieved its aim at the relatively low cost of under 500 casualties, taking control of the high ground and the main road to Bayeux and Caen below it.

Also on 11 July, the 29th and 35th Divisions were to attack and take the high ground north of Saint-Lô: Hill 122 and the Martinville Ridge. The 29th's 116th Infantry ran into heavy fire from Hill 122 but the opposition caved in as 2nd Division took Hill 192 and the 116th quickly reached the Martinville Ridge. The German forces ahead of them had themselves suffered dreadfully. Blumenson cites figures of 3rd Fallschirmjäger

Above Left: The approach to Saint-Lô.

Left: The attack on Hill 192.

Above: Tanks and infantry make a careful crossing of the open space between the hedgerows near Pont-Hébert.

Below: Maj-Gen Manton Eddy (front right of the jeep), commander of 9th Infantry Division. Photo taken on 26 July, northwest of Saint-Lô at Les Champs-de-Losque (per Jean Pallud in *Rückmarsch!*).

Division being at no more than 35 percent strength and the supporting Kampfgruppe from 353rd Division down to 180 men from a thousand. Nevertheless, that night the Fallschirmjäger set up position astride the Martinville Ridge and the next day 29th Division lost 500 men, mainly to artillery and mortar fire: this meant a thousand in two days. By 13 July 29th Division lacked the strength to take Hill 112 by itself and so General Corlett turned to the 35th Division, which had made only slight gains since the 11th. With 30th Division making ground along one side of the Vire, the 35th attacked down the other, taking Emélie. A task force including two companies of 737th Tank Battalion and a platoon of 654th TD Battalion took Hill 122. The division withstood a serious counterattack on 16 July, but held. It was the beginning of the end.

The Germans also felt that the writing was on the wall. Seventh Armee asked for permission to withdraw, and just at this point, on 17 July, Heeresgruppe B's commander, Erwin Rommel, was badly wounded when his staff car was strafed. OB West von Kluge took over. The German troops left Saint-Lô with only a rearguard.

On the morning of 18 July, led out by 115th Infantry of 29th Division, General 'Dutch' Cota's task force entered the city at 18:00. That evening Gen Charles H. Gerhardt told Gen Corlett: 'I have the honor to announce to the Corps Commander that Task Force C of the 29th Division secured the city of Saint-Lô after 43 days of continual combat from the beaches to Saint-Lô.'

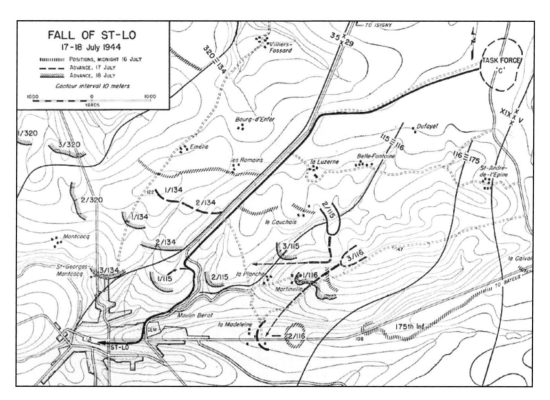

Above: GIs of 35th Infantry Division who landed over Omaha Beach on 5–7 July advance towards their position on the right of the 29th Infantry Division northwest of Saint-Lô. The 137th Infantry Regiment went in the direction of La Meauffe, the 320th to Le Carillon and the 134th was held in reserve in Villiers-Fossard. The photograph was taken before the 35th went into action on 11 July.

Below: Hill 192 is a commanding high ground feature outside Saint-Lô and 2nd Infantry Division had been sitting on its northern slopes since 17 June, giving the 352. Infanterie-Division defenders a long time to ready the defence of their hedgerows. On 11 July, following a rolling barrage, 2nd Infantry took the hill in spite of the stubborn defence.

Artillery was used extensively in the bocage battles. 30th Division artillery fired 9,000 rounds on 11 July; 3rd Armored 6,000. The barrage of 9 July—as the American Forces in Action series title on *Saint-Lô* has it—was something 'never seen before.' On 15 July attacking Hill 122, 92nd Chemical Mortar Bn fired 7,000 rounds and 35th Division Artillery fired 11,000.

More than 25,000 rounds were fired by the artillery battalions—around 300 rounds per 105mm gun. The 50,000th round would be fired during the battle for Saint-Lô.

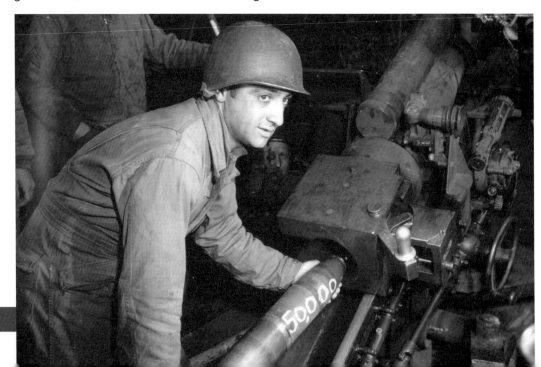

Above: The batteries positioned on Hill 122 had pounded the 29th Infantry Division as they tried to advance along the Martinville Ridge. Hill 122 was taken by 134th and 137th Regiments of the 35th Infantry on 16 July after two days of fighting. This photo was taken the following day.

Above: This M10 is that of Capt Sidney A. Vincent of B Co of the 803rd TD Bn which was KO'd by an 88mm on the morning of 18 July during the attack on Saint-Lô by a task force organized by Brig-Gen. Norman D. Cota.

Above Right: Troops of the 29th Infantry Division enter Saint-Lô.

Right: An M5A1 of D Co, 747th Tank Bn advances through the rubble in Saint-Lô, 19 July.

Mines were a continual problem. In Lessay, a village of only 2,000 people, VIII Corps engineer units removed more than 300 booby traps one afternoon in July. To help, the corps' engineer teams showed the tankers of the 4th and 6th Armd Divs how to cope with mine removal, giving demonstrations with real mines.

Above: Mine problems east of Saint-Lô on 20 July. An ammunition carrier struck a mine causing the need for mine clearance on the verges.

Right: Telltale black smoke rises from a mine explosion on 19 July—this time it immobilised an M4.

Above Left: Bulldozers in Saint-Lô. Everything left behind, including bodies and equipment, had to be scoured for booby traps.

Below Left: The 29th Infantry in Saint-Lô. The division suffered heavily on its journey from Omaha, suffering some 8,000 casualties.

Above: *Hun Chaser* of the HQ Co, 747th Tank Bn part of the Cota Task Force of the 29th Infantry. On 18 July in front of the Sherman, a tanker in a characteristic helmet and binoculars, checks out the environment. The remaining tower on the Church of Notre-Dame would be destroyed by a German bombardment that night.

Below: Maj Thomas D. Howie, commander of the 3/116th Infantry Regiment, 29th Infantry, was killed by a mortar shell. His men carried his body into the city and placed him on the ruins of the bell-tower of Sainte-Croix church. Major Howie has passed into legend as the 'Major of Saint-Lô'.

60148

Views of Saint-Lô during and after the battle: night view showing fires from bombing (**Left**); wrecked SdKfz 231 8-Rad (wheel) reconnaissance vehicle (**Above**); aerial view taken 28 July (**Below**).

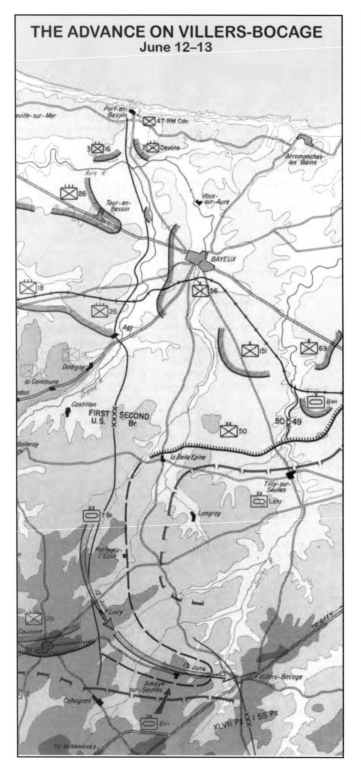

THE ADVANCE ON VILLERS-BOCAGE
June 12–13

The advance on Villers-Bocage. The withdrawal of the German 352nd Division led to the swift advance to Caumont by US 1st Infantry Division (see p.57). Alongside, British 7th Armoured Division advanced towards Villers-Bocage.

Chapter Seven

The British in the Bocage

It's easy to forget that the bocage stretched from the Cotentin to Falaise and that fighting in the hedgerows was not simply the preserve of the US forces. While the 'Battle of the Hedgerows' has come to mean US First Army's struggle from the beachheads to Saint-Lô, in fact both US First Army and British Second had to contend with similar terrain.

Following D-Day, there were limited gains in the British Army sector. To the east 6th Airborne Division held off counterattacks and ensured that the flank of British Second Army was unmolested. In front of Caen, Montgomery—in Bradley's words—'was spending his reputation in a bitter siege against the old university city of Caen. For three weeks he had rammed his troops against those Panzer divisions he had deliberately drawn toward that city as part of our Allied strategy of diversion in the Normandy campaign.' He was able to do so because, in the same way that Bradley did on the First Army front, he held the initiative, forcing the Germans to react to his attacks and leaving them no chance to pull together a sufficiently large force to counterattack and turn the tables.

The first significant British operation after the landings was Operation Perch, an attempt to advance to the southeast of Caen (the other pincer movement on the east of the Orne having been held by German counterattacks). Three days into the operation the Allies became aware of the gap that had been created by the disintegration of 352nd Infantry Division. This allowed US 1st Infantry to advance to Caumont. British XXX Corps unleashed the Desert Rats, sending 7th Armoured Division in a right hook towards Villers-Bocage and Caen. The Germans sent the Tigers of SS-sPzAbt 101 to help retrieve the position and they met at Villers-Bocage (see next page).

Similar circumstances on 30 July—the withdrawal of 2nd Panzer Divison—left a gap south of Caumont. Taking advantage of this, and in order to fix German forces in the east, Operation Bluecoat involved XXX Corps—43rd (Wessex), 50th (Northumbrian), and 7th Armoured divisions—and VIII Corps led by the most dynamic of the British armoured divisions in Normandy—the 11th under 'Pip' Roberts—along with Guards Armoured and 15th Scottish. 11th Armoured found a bridge across the Souleuvre enabling it to advance deep into enemy territory, withstanding strong counterattacks which helped wear down the German armoured formations in the area—vitally important as it helped weaken the German 7 August counterattack, Operation Lüttich.

Villers-Bocage is best-remembered for the exploits of SS-Obersturmführer Michael Wittmann. He and his unit disabled or knocked-out a number of light tanks, halftracks, scout cars and several Cromwells and Shermans, before Wittmann's tank was disabled by a 6-pdr antitank gun. The damage is usually assessed as 13–14 tanks, two antitank guns and 13–15 transport vehicles: an outstanding success. However, as a poster boy for the Waffen-SS, Wittmann's exploits were inflated both at the time and subsequently. Wittmann didn't take part in the battle that afternoon when the Tigers of his CO, SS-Hauptsturmführer Rolf Möbius, and supporting tanks of Panzer Lehr were ambushed in the town by Lt. Bill Cotton of the 4th CLY, losing six Tigers and a number of PzKpfw IVs.

1 The wrecked British column on the road to Point 213—a close-up of one of the three Recce Troop Stuarts.

2 Knocked out Sherman OP from K Bty, 5RHA. Note the wooden gun barrel.

3 Wittmann's attack destroyed the advance guard of 7th Armoured.

4 Tiger 121 knocked out on the rue Pasteur.

5 Bill Cotton (far left) and his crew after the battle. He received an MC for bravery. Note he's wearing a Luftwaffe jacket complete with Iron Cross!

Above: British armour in the bocage. Operations such as Bluecoat led to considerable casualties as the Germans defended in depth in the hedgerows and hills of Suisse Normande.

Right: The so-called 'Charge of the Bull'—a reference to 11th Armoured's bull insignia—started with Operation Bluecoat on 30 July when the division took St-Martin-des-Besaces. Recce units discovered a surviving bridge over the Souleuvre river and 11th Armoured charged over, liberating Le Bény-Bocage on 1 August. Contentiously warned away from relatively undefended Vire (in the American zone) when elements of 11th Armoured were close, the division advanced southward but had to withstand counterattacks from 5 August by 9th SS-Panzer Division (*Hohenstaufen*), elements of 21st Panzer Division, and the Tigers of sPzAbt 102. With a confused battlefield—the Suisse Normande is like the bocage with steep hills—and infiltration by small enemy units, the Royal Artillery was instrumental in holding the line long enough for reinforcements—in the form of British 3rd Inf Div—to arrive. On 6 August, 43rd (Wessex) Division and 13th/18th Hussars took the biggest of the Suisse Normande's hills, Mount Pinçon, after heavy fighting.

Men of the 6th Royal Scots Fusiliers, 15th (Scottish) Division, fire from their positions in a sunken lane during Operation Epsom. Stuart Hills remembers the fighting west of Caen:

'The bocage could be turned into a veritable fortress, and indeed it was ... The Allied tanks would have preferred to stick to the high ground and better roads, but the Germans held most of the high ground and had their 88mm guns placed to cover the main roads with devastating fire. So tanks, in their key role of supporting infantry, had to go with them into the narrow lanes.'

He then goes on to point out all the problems that this caused, not least the 15th Scottish losses: 2,331 killed, wounded, or missing in the operation.

Further Reading

After the Battle: magazines and books, especially Pallud and Ramsey (see below).

American Forces in Action series: *Saint-Lô;* CMH reprint of War Department, 1946.

Balkoski, Joseph: *Beyond the Beachhead: The 29th Division in Normandy;* Stackpole Books, 1989.

Blumenson, Martin: *US Army in World War II The European Theater of Operations Break-out and Pursuit;* CMH, 1961.

Bradley, Omar N.: *A Soldier's Story;* Henry Holt & Co., 1951.

Carafino, James Jay: *After D-Day;* Lynne Rienner Publishers Inc., 2000.

Daugherty, Leo: *The Battle of the Hedgerows;* Ian Allan Ltd, 2001.

Doubler, Capt Michael D.: *Busting the Bocage: American Combined Arms Operations in France, 16 June–31 July 1944;* Combat Studies Institue, 1988.

Dugan, Haynes W.: *Spearhead in the West;* Turner Publishing Company, 1991.

Harrison, Gordon A.: *US Army in World War II The European Theater of Operations Cross-Channel Attack;* CMH, Washington, 1993.

Hills, Stuart: *By Tank into Normandy;* Cassel, 2002.

Isby, David C. [Ed.]: *Fighting the Breakout;* Frontline Books, 2015.

Pallud, Jean-Paul: *Rückmarsch! The German Retreat from Normandy Then and Now;* After the Battle, 2006.

Pamp, Capt Frederick E., Jr: *From Normandy to the Elbe*: XIX Corps history.

Ramsey, Winston G.: *D-Day Then and Now* vol 2; After the Battle, 1995.

Reardon, Mark J. [ed.]: *Defending Fortress Europe;* The Aberjona Press, 2015.

Smith, Steven: *Spearhead 10: 2nd Armored Division 'Hell on Wheels';* Ian Allan Ltd, 2003.

Third Armored Division: *Spearhead in the West;* The Battery Press, 1980.

Whitlock, Flint: *The Fighting First;* Westview Press, 2004.

Yates, Peter: *Battle Zone Normandy 10: Battle for Caen;* Alan Sutton, 2004.

Zaloga, Stephen: *Cherbourg 1944;* Osprey Publishing, 2015.